THRONE OF GAMES:

KING FERGIE, LORD MOYES & THE SEASON OF GRIM DEATH

Story by Paul Harrie (House Mancunia)
Artwork by Oliver Ninnis (Freeman)

First published October 2014
Freight Books
49-53 Virginia Street
Glasgow, G1 1TS
www.freightbooks.co.uk

A CIP catalogue reference for this book is available from the British Library

ISBN 978-1-908754-87-5
eISBN 978-1-908754-88-2

Printed and bound in Poland

Principal Characters

KING FERGIE
The Old God

LORD MOYES, HOUSE EVERTONIA
later Ruler of House Mancunia

LORD GIGGS
Prince of Welsh Dragons

LORD ROONEY
a rebellious knight

TRIPLE FINGER
the Chairman of the Board
of Counsellers

GRAND MAESTER
Bobby Charlton

VAN GAAL
New King of the North

PROLOGUE

1. THE WALL

ither side of Hadrian's Wall are two very different worlds. South of it lies the Twenty Kingdoms, a rich and wasteful place populated by thieves, media pundits and no shortage of pretenders. But north of it is another land entirely, occupied for centuries by fierce tribes known to hostile outsiders as 'the Jocks'. Though a small nation, absent from World Cups for a thousand years, these 'Jocks' are famous for producing fearless Leaders of Men like no other place on land or sea. Once such leader is Lord Fergie, a man with a furious temper and an appetite for fine wines…

BOOK ONE
THE THRONE OF GAMES

2. THE LION AND THE ROSE

ailing from the bleak hamlet of Govan, a haunted outpost of the once-powerful shipping port of Glasgae, Lord Fergie marches three hundred leagues north of his hometown, with a rose between his teeth, to take Aberdonia. This is a little known, glory-free zone near the land of ice, where the rain falls sideways and the hearts of women are said to be made of granite.

New keeper The Mountain's unnaturally strong grip costs the club another £100

*The Chairman shows the management team the
boardroom's new performance-related moon door*

3. THE OLD GOD

ut great leaders can transform even dunghills into pots of gold. As ruler of Aberdonia, Lord Fergie wins unlikely victories at home and abroad. His fame spreads, and reaches powerful ears in other lands. Soon the man they call 'The Old God' is coveted by many on the other side of Hadrian's Wall, in the part of the Twenty Kingdoms known as The North West. One particular man, the Chairman of the Board, holds the purse strings at the once-great empire of Mancunia. Advised by Grand Maester Bobby Charlton and haunted by the ghost of George Best, Mancunia has been trophy-less for decades but is beginning, once again, to dream of greatness.

4. THE NORTH WEST

ne dark night, after sacking Ron Atkinson, the Chairman of the Board of Mancunia sets out to track Lord Fergie down. He spends weeks on horseback, travelling through the wilds of the North West, then the border towns either side of Hadrian's Wall, then the mountains. Like many soft southerners, he finds these lands a mystery. The Chairman sends a raven home to his wife: 'Darling, these chaps are a curious bunch. Half of them speak endlessly about 'independence from the Twenty Kingdoms', the other half equally endlessly about avoiding it. Apparently they've been doing so for 300 years.' Then he mounts his steed once more.

5. THE WATCHERS

ventually The Chairman reaches the gates of Aberdonia, his exhausted servants carrying sacks of gold behind him. On arrival, he asks the knights of the realm to take him to 'he who is made of fire and blood'. The meeting with Lord Fergie is short. After being presented with the gold, he swears a new oath and abandons his castle at Aberdonia, riding over Hadrian's Wall at once to conquer new lands, claim his rightful place as a great king and, most importantly, to 'knock Liverpool off their fucking perch'.

6. GOOD KING FERGIE

hich he does. Fergie may be the most scheming and ruthless King in history, a liar, vagabond and furious Holder of Unfounded Grudges, but he is also a born winner. He chooses allies wisely and enemies even more so. He is also an expert in what the vanquished call 'squeaky bum time', those crucial moments at the end of a battle where reputations are made and lost, and extra minutes spring from nowhere. Such talents are more valuable than all the gold in the Twenty Kingdoms, and King Fergie's charges taste victory time and again. The people sing his name in Old Traffordia, Mancunia's Theatre of Dreams. (Though not as much as Fergie would like.)

*The old king spends his days drinking wine
in the company of media whores*

House Baratheon's fans were excited by their new signing – a <u>classically</u> trained actor

7. THEATRE OF DREAMS

n the coming seasons many heroes are born and die in Old Traffordia. The door revolves fast. The names of the latest warriors are chanted by the faithful one week then forgotten by those same peasants the next, often before their bodies are even cold, or moved on to Sunderland – but through it all, King Fergie rules on. And Gods help anyone who resists him!

8. MY STORY

hat includes his own charges. Should they be caught telling of their adventures in the taverns or whorehouses of Alderley Edge, and should their words displease him, King Fergie is wont to throw knights in the dungeon, or sell them abroad to the highest bidder. Condemned to sit alongside fools on ITV's Seat of Impotence, the murderous, one-eyed cut-throat Keano has had many years to reflect on what might have been if he'd not questioned the King. He's not alone. The grass of the Theatre of Dreams is littered with blood and corpses, and for the warriors who fail, it truly is a Theatre of Nightmares.

*Beyond the wall, undersoil wildfire was being
tested with mixed results*

At free kicks the Northerners' wall did its job time and again

9. THE ENDLESS REIGN

ing Fergie's name is legend throughout the Twenty Kingdoms, and his instrument of torture, The Hairdryer, is feared by all who serve under him. With a furious energy belying his years, King Fergie clings on night and day to the seat they call the 'Iron Throne of Games'. It is said that once, in 2003, he grew tired of the pressures of power, and tried to relinquish the throne, only for his queen to return him there, in the hope of 'keeping the auld bugger out from under my feet, for a few more years at least.' So he remains a little longer, all his subjects now aware of just where the power really lies in the kingdom.

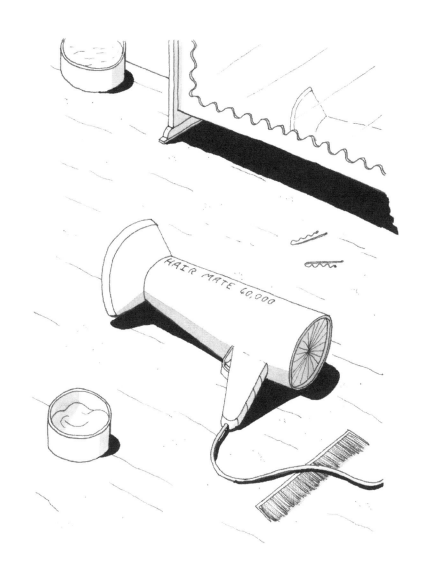

10. THE TAVERNS OF MANCUNIA

ing Fergie has now ruled over House Mancunia for as long as any living soul can remember, and some in Mancunia even believe he will live forever. In the taverns around the city walls, they talk of a long-ago time known as 'the 80s', when Sky Sports didn't exist, the riches of the Premier League were a distant dream, and House Mancunia was laughed at in the homes of Liverpudlia. But it's hard to believe in the truth of such a world, so distant does it seem.

*Due to the unusual shape of the new World Cup Ball officials
hoped its performance would be excitingly unpredictable*

11. THE LAWS OF GODS AND MEN

ince they were boys, followers of King Fergie have known nothing but glory. And while he prospers, other Houses suffer. The noble knight Gerrard has no league titles to his name, for example, while King Fergie's most loyal and long-serving knight, the Welsh dragon Prince Giggsy, has thirteen. It's hardly fair now, is it? But then, the laws of Gods and men are anything but fair. The Twenty Kingdoms are a lawless place. Men will claw their brothers' eyes out, if it means earning an extra ten grand a week.

12. REAL MANCUNIA

here are other powerful seats in the Twenty Kingdoms too. Oil-rich House Stamford. The once-relevant Francophile House Arsene. The ever-failing House of Spurs. There is even a rival kingdom within Mancunia, the men who call themselves Ci-teh. But their followers skulk in the shadows, shame-faced, talking in hushed tones about 'the Real Mancunia' – since the arrival of King Fergie in the North West they have barely won a silver coin, never mind a battle worth crowing about. In the taverns under King Fergie, they laugh at the idea that Ci-teh could ever have dominion over them, and charge their glasses once more.

*There was a buzz amongst the Targaryen fans about
three exciting prospects in the youth team*

13. THE SHEIKS' ARRIVAL

ut one day Ci-teh are conquered by the cash-rich 'Sheikhs', a powerful tribe who march all the way from the deserts of Middle-Essos to the Twenty Kingdoms, and whose traditions are as mysterious as those of the Dothraki, or the French. These 'Sheikhs' rarely address their new subjects, and when they do, they speak with their wallets. They have promised and delivered not only great riches but also a brave warrior called Vincent Kompany, the Hound, who has a face they say is too hideous to look upon but is nevertheless worth more than a dozen Patrice Evras. King Fergie complains of his 'noisy neighbours'. Times are changing in the Twenty Kingdoms. And soon, a man called Davie Moyes will have reason to curse those changes.

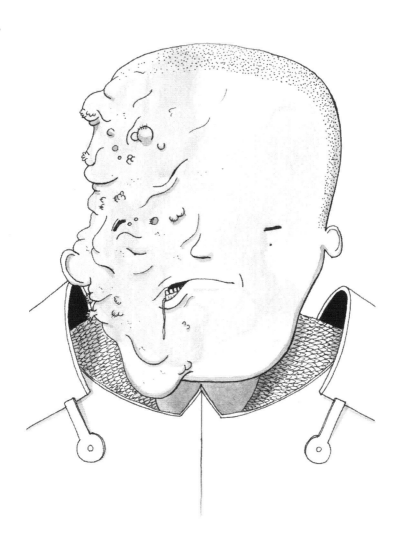

BOOK TWO

A HANDOVER OF KINGS

14. OATHKEEPER

 n another outpost of the bitterly cold North West, Lord Davie Moyes and his assistants from lowly Preston North End have stormed the castle of Evertonia, a mere forty leagues from Mancunia. His early followers call him the Oathkeeper, as he is a Godsfearing man, who has forsworn women and wine in the name of a higher cause – miserable abstinence. Moyes too was born and raised in the chilly climate of Glasgae, that town that seems to sprout tough managers the way some kings sprout bastards. Moyes, just like the leader of House Mancunia, is of humble origins. King Fergie hears of the younger man, notes his rise, and is careful not to make another enemy.

15. A MINOR KINGDOM

vertonia does enjoy a number of small victories, but it never touches silverware, not even a League Cup. Still, the name of Lord Moyes rings moderately loud in his land, and the people treat him as one of their own. It is even said, in some quarters, that if he were given the gold of, say, House Mancunia, Lord Moyes could build a truly great and noble kingdom, vanquishing dark forces far and wide and bringing bread to the poor. But alas, the Evertonian coffers are empty. So, the Europa League it is then.

Fined for being late for training, Lannister's keeper wondered if the new disciplinary regime might prove counter-productive

16. A LONG WAIT

oyes has long held greater ambitions than this. He has now ruled Evertonia for one long winter which has lasted, it seems, forever - a time in which Evertonia have occasionally appeared in the Champions League but never got past the qualifying rounds. His most celebrated knights have deserted him for bigger clubs. He's been made to eat scraps. Meanwhile, at court in Mancunia, King Fergie hosts banquet after banquet, and his reign rumbles on like a long storm, a haunting echo, or a never-ending name day celebration.

17. THE KINGSROAD

ord Moyes marches down the Kingsroad once a year with his troops to The Royal Court at Mancunia, at King Fergie's pleasure, to joust badly, pay cringing tribute and partake of a cup of wine or three with his Master after the festivities. Then he mounts his horse and returns, humbled, to his poor little corner of The North West, usually with a longer injury list. And then there are the battles on his own turf.

*Teams from the twenty kingdoms had to guard against scouts
from White Walkers FC stealing their best young talent*

18. THE POINTY END

hen King Fergie comes to Evertonia, he insults the locals by not even staying long enough to bloody the pointy end of his sword. He simply arrives, snatches his three points and heads back to the castle at Mancunia. Lord Moyes looks on with green eyes at this fellow man of Glasgae, who has risen so high and remained there so long. He cannot help but dream. What if the throne of Mancunia was his? But no, such a thing would never happen. They'd probably want a king who'd actually won something.

19. STEP ASIDE, OLD MAN

Yet more seasons pass. King Fergie is now crag-faced and ancient, and is looking for someone to pass his kingdom over to that he can trust. His face is now almost as red as his Bannermans' standard, and he dreams of retiring to his chamber to write his memoirs – a great, fat book in which he will detail every traitor, every glory, every loyal knight and dishonourable scandal, conveniently missing out his own. Then he will tour the book all over the world – except, perhaps, Merseyside. Meanwhile, who might he pass his legacy on to? Perhaps someone from the same stock? A fellow member of the Glasgae Mafia perhaps?

*There was grumbling amongst fans over the new knight's
purchase of several top of the range carts*

20. DARK MAGIC

eanwhile, across the narrow sea in Madrid, there lies in wait the flamboyant Lord Mourinho, an illusionist and magician hailing from the obscure Portuguese peoples, who are certainly handsome but, according to King Fergie, whose 'wine tastes like pish'. One of few whose glory can compete with the Old God's power, the self-proclaimed 'Special One' Mourinho lets it be known through his agent, and several blatantly obvious newspaper interviews, that he covets the Iron Throne of Games.

21. BREAKER OF CHAINS

ut Mourinho is not destined to sit on it. Ever the master of surprise, King Fergie shocks the realm by inviting Lord Moyes to his palace in secret to share a horn of ale, announcing his immediate retirement and anointing him as the new King of House Mancunia. 'As you command it, my King,' says Moyes, bending the knee, trembling with disbelief. 'Oh but you are the King now, Davie,' says the elder of the two, breaking out into a knowing smile. 'But beware, my chosen one: the game is ruthless. Here, you either win or you die. There's no question aboot that. No question aboot that at all.'

22. A PEOPLE MUST OBEY

oon after, Lord Fergie breaks the news of the succession to his people, instructing them to be loyal to their new leader for six winters and perhaps more, dependent on results. The people throw feasts in King Fergie's name, celebrating his long reign, throwing up statues in his image. As for new King Davie, the people have little choice but to welcome him. The decision has already been made, by the Old God, who no one is brave enough to question.

23. BEWARE THE RAVEN

cross the narrow sea, a raven brings Lord Mourinho the news of the man who has taken the throne he believed to be rightfully his. Mourinho howls alone in his kingdom from sundown to sunrise – 'Why? Why? Lowly Moyes is not worthy!' - though he later denies this in the media. Soon after, he is invited to rule House Stamford, the land of ill-gotten riches in the south of the Twenty Kingdoms, where he ruled as a younger man. Never go back, say the sages. Especially to Roman Abramovich. But the Russian's riches speak louder than the sages, and Mourinho glumly packs his bags.

24. FIRST OF HIS NAME

o Lord Moyes is now King Davie Moyes of Mancunia, the First of his Name. He is given a golden crown to wear, also a Standard from supporters in the Royal Court, the motto reading 'The Chosen One'. Moyes turns to the skies and swears an oath: 'In the name of the Old God and the New, a recently appointed three-headed Chairman called Triple Finger, I pledge every ounce of my strength to make Nani's performances consistent!' The faithful wonder if such a thing is possible. Perhaps it is? After all, they do live in a world of miracles.

25. LONG LIVE GOOD KING DAVIE

The next day, King Davie sets off on a tour of Thailand, Australia, Japan and Hong Kong, good wishes ringing in his ears and gold coins rattling in his pockets. In his grasp he holds a piece of paper, signed by Fergie himself, giving him six cycles to build a new empire. The Old God has instructed the people, 'Your job now is to stand by our new King.' He even has Fergie's great warrior Prince Giggsy by his side, the silver-haired knight accepting a coaching position while still fighting for the cause on the battlefield. It's all falling into place, thinks King Davie. What could possibly go wrong?

There was a degree of suspicion over Baratheon FC's new Technical Director's leech-based decision-making regime

*As another battle approaches, a tavern fight breaks out over
Squire Panini's famous knight collectable miniatures*

BOOK THREE
THE STORM OF SHITE

26. THE IRON DUGOUT

At the start of the season The Chosen One takes his place in the Iron Dugout for his first battle with his Team of Champions, the finest warriors in the Twenty Kingdoms. His heart swells as they hammer the mighty Wigan Athletic 2-0 in the south – in the aftermath, Moyes promises 'a long summer of peace and plenty'. It's going to be a breeze. Next, they batter the Welsh on their own soil, the sages saying that Moyes's reign will be just like his predecessor's – merciless, and all-powerful. The Kingdoms quake, Mourinho curses his luck and the odds on House Mancunia retaining their title shrink at Paddy Power.

27. CRIPPLES, BASTARDS & BROKEN THINGS

ut peace is short-lived. From his poor view at Evertonia, the knights of the Mancunian realm had always appeared invincible to King Davie. But one day during sword practice he realizes that what seemed from the outside to be a rich army of supermen is in fact a bankrupt band of the ageing and the infirm. Lord Ferdinand of Rio is headless, he notices, though still barking orders to others. The glass-jawed Van Persie, he now sees, is carried on the back of Vidic, the brute who can speak only one word, his own name. Moyes thinks to himself: how did Fergie make them winners? His forehead begins to twitch, and when he thinks of the future, his eyes bulge, ever so slightly.

28. THE NIGHT LANDS

n the coming weeks, Moyes's sleeping hours are full of terrors. Good King Fergie had inspired both love and fear in the people, he had been known to change the seasons, even poison the hearts of his enemies with 'mind games'. Having long ago pledged to forego all but earnest toil, Moyes has no such access to the black arts. In his nightmares, that famous puce face hovers over him, screaming, as King Davie imagines himself stumbling through the night lands, lost, without a half decent holding midfielder for company. Sometimes Moyes bolts upright in his bed, sweating: 'Come back Paul Scholes!' he cries out, still unconscious. 'Just for one more season!'

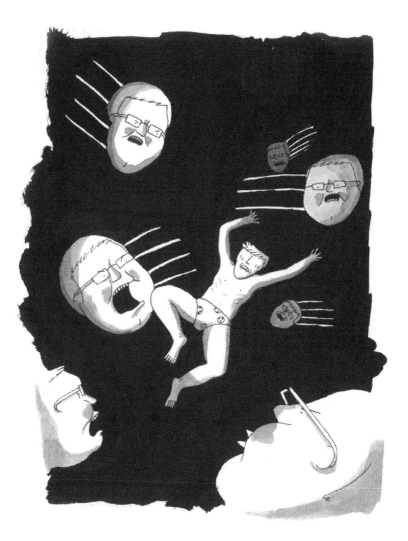

29. THE NEW REGIME

oyes's waking hours hold no peace either. Soon follows an interminable, costly stalemate with Mourinho's House Stamford, then a defeat to the Scousers of Liverpudlia, new pretenders to the throne who Good King Fergie famously put to the sword so many times. In the new House Mancunia, men of honour are hard to come by, and there are murmurings of revolution in the ranks. Even the loyal Prince Giggsy is known to be sharpening his blade. And what for, wonders King Davie, if not to stab me in the back?

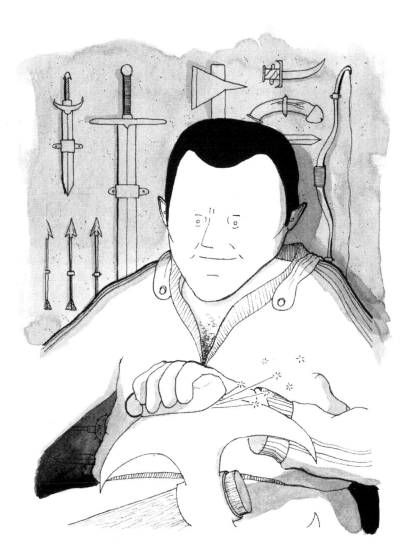

30. TROUBLE IN THE KINGDOM

Only days later, Moyes's knights, who are again without their eternally injured talisman Van Persie, are put to the sword by Ci-teh. On this day of abject humiliation their fierce local rivals smell weakness and attack, their own new King, Pelligrini of Santiago, ripping out the heart of Ashley Young and devouring it as a show of strength in front of the baying crowd. For the first time, a few brave souls standing at the statue of the Old God begin to speak those unspeakable words: Oh shit, should we have appointed Mourinho?

31. THE NEWS

umours abound in the kingdom, some so foul that not even The Sun will print them. One afternoon, so they say, Van Persie is pushed out of a window after spotting the Sisters Neville indulging in unnatural acts – though this is later hushed up in the media. Meanwhile, the rabid phone-ins of the realm hum with the sound of doubters, spouting off after a couple of pints about how their grandmothers are better warriors than Tom Cleverley. King Davie has seen contracts ripped up before, and in moments of weakness, he imagines his own cast onto the fire by Triple Finger.

32. THE ENEMIES

s the season warms up, Citeh, Liverpudlia, and House Stamford grow powerful, the three battling for supremacy. Meanwhile King Moyes needs to strengthen his depleted ranks, but can't persuade anyone to do so. Head bowed low, he ends up at the gates of his old kingdom on transfer deadline day, begging to be granted access to Leighton Baines. But no, he is refused, leaving Moyes to return with nothing but empty pockets and the knight they call 'The Clown-Haired One'. Seeing the new arrival ride over the hill from Evertonia, Van Persie says to The Knight With No Legs, Michael Carrick, 'Hark, look who comes to join us! If this is all the gaffer can bring us, we really are totally fucked.'

As the ref makes another dubious decision, the Eerie stadium resounds with the Arryn supporters' chant, 'Make the bad man fly!'

*After another mid-table finish, Lannister United's manager
decides it's time for a squad clear-out*

33. A MAN WITHOUT HONOUR

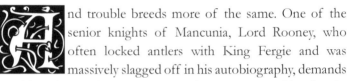nd trouble breeds more of the same. One of the senior knights of Mancunia, Lord Rooney, who often locked antlers with King Fergie and was massively slagged off in his autobiography, demands a golden ransom from King Davie for his continued loyalty. Or else, he says, he'll defect to House Stamford in the South where the wages are better, the chances of silverware higher, and the WAGS are more accommodating.

House Tully's top striker decides to forgo wine, whores and milk of the poppy - for pre-season at least

34. A MAN WITH HONOUR

The Gods-fearing Moyes is horrified by Rooney's bribery, as he is with the club-faced one's attitude to the fairer sex. (Alas, Rooney is not alone in the Twenty Kingdoms in his primitive attitudes to gender politics. Even Prince Giggsy turned out to be a love rat.) As the temperature drops in Mancunia and results continue to go awry, King Moyes is forced to accede to Lord Rooney's demands, promising him the role of Hand of the King once Vidic has been packed off to Serie A in Italy, the League Where Slow Defenders Go to Die.

35. POWER LIES WHERE MEN BELIEVE IT LIES

ooney agrees to the deal, stays, and returns to the bloody business of war, but the message it sends out is clear. Is Moyes really in charge of his men, ask the sages at Talksport? Or are the men in charge of him? Worse, are they still loyal to King Fergie, whose name the people of Mancunia sing every Saturday and occasional Tuesday, also some Wednesdays, and the odd Sunday, if that particular game is live on ESPN?

36. GARDEN OF BONES

Though there are occasional victories for Moyes and his men, there are more defeats, too many, and most of them on the sacred home soil of Mancunia. What was once a Theatre of Dreams has truly become a garden of bones. These days, great rivals come to court and mock the reign of King Davie, torturing his so-called 'champions' for fun. Even forces who are not considered great rivals, or considered at all, leave with the heads of Mancunian knights, freshly plucked from their shoulders and ready to present to their kings.

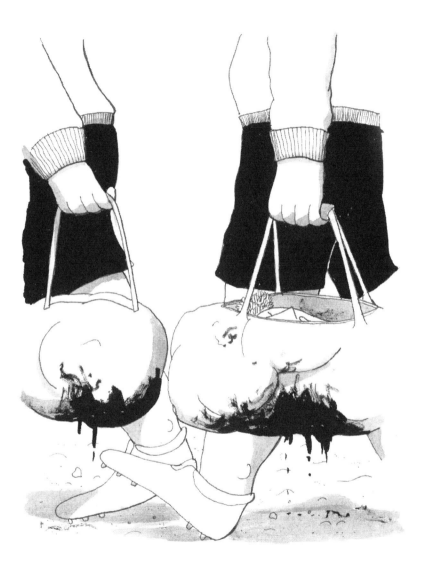

37. THE RISE OF EVERTONIA

umiliation piles upon humiliation one day in the depths of winter, when the new Evertonian troops of King Martinez come to Old Traffordia and escape with victory. Moyes's old charges have not tasted victory in Mancunia since before the long reign of King Fergie and one sage, Jamie Redknapp, is heard to say, 'Literally, it like, literally, literally can't get worse.' Then they are defeated by Newcastle. King Davie says to Prince Giggsy, 'We'd better sign Juan Mata, and fast, or our heads will end up on spikes'. Giggsy rubs his hands together, saying, 'Perhaps yours will, Your Grace, perhaps yours will.'

38. WINTER IS COMING

he corpses of this latest humiliation all around him, Moyes calls his troops together on the battlefield to make a desperate appeal. He summons his cup-bearer Phil Neville. Then, glass charged, eyes bulging, he calls on his depleted ranks to remember their sworn vows, and, come next battle, to 'curse and fight until your hearts are done pumping'. 'They may forget your names,' he cries out, voice hoarse, 'they may forget you ever lived, but they will know there are trophies in the cabinet because you gave your lives for House Mancunia!' The knights cheer and drain their glasses, but soon they are defeated by Norwich. And Spurs. And later, even by Stoke City. Truly, the grimmest of winters has arrived.

*Young club chairman Joffrey decides to test the veracity
of House Lannister fans' claim to be 'die-hards'*

*The imp Ser Messi had more than enough in his
locker to make up for his lack of height*

BOOK FOUR
A Feast for Sky Sports

39. THE ROYAL COURT

hese are Mancunia's very darkest days. Doubters even suggest Fergie still controls the kingdom, whispering orders in Moyes's ear. Well, the Old God would have never put up with such insubordination at a post-match press conference, but Moyes only twitches grimly as he insists a good leader takes good counsel. 'Sure, I pick up the phone from time to time,' he tells the journalists. 'So what?' Yet King Davie's cheeks turn a hellish red. And after the next mauling, this time in the F.A. Cup, he can be heard muttering darkly about how 'traitors will feel my sword at their throats before long' and how he thinks 'we actually played quite well today'. The journos thumb their noses, sharpen their quills, then set about the next punning headline.

The team's new Valyrian steel toe caps gave extra purchase in the wet

As chants of 'who's the bastard in the black?' rang round the stadium, referee Snow realised his surname was a gift to the fans

40. THE MAD KING

Just when it seems things can't get worse, the knights of Mancunia collapse to Sunderland in a bloody horror show, which King Moyes describes as 'surely a bit of a turning point'. By now whisperings in court have grown into open mockery, no longer delivered behind the hands – have the ravens plucked out Moyes's eyes and replaced them with dragon eggs? Is he cursed by the witches, doomed to fail and fail until House Mancunia is nothing but dust and carcasses? His kinder subjects call him 'Half-Manager'. The rest call him 'The Mad King'. So mad that he can't see just how rotten his court has become.

41. THE GRAND MAESTER ADVISES CAUTION

ntil now the new Chairman of the Board, Triple Finger, a three-headed bloodsucker from House Glazer, has looked mercifully on Moyes. There's been talk of rebuilding, regrouping - lots of words beginning with 'r'. But now shame blights the kingdom, the treasure chests have been looted, and Champions League qualification is impossible. Triple Finger agrees to meet Grand Maester Charlton for a lunch of prawn sandwiches in a Salford alehouse to discuss matters. 'The mad king may not be long for this world,' he says, drawing a finger across his throat. As ever, the Grand Maester advises caution. As ever, he is ignored.

42. IT'S WIN OR DIE

fter another defeat at home to Ci-teh, who now seem to be heading for the ultimate glory, and another mauling at the hands of Liverpudlia which the people are already referring to as 'The Red Wedding', Triple Finger summons King Moyes and delivers his ultimatum: from now on, it's win or die. Will you, Davie Moyes of Glasgae, be able to return this kingdom to glory immediately, asks the Chairman? Wild-eyed, furrowed of brow, pupils almost popping from their sockets, King Moyes mutters: 'We can still win the league…our defences are strong…and there's no doubt about it, Triple Finger, Chris Smalling is worth fifty million…'

*Play is halted for several minutes after another
direwolf runs onto the pitch*

43. THE WRONG ONE

ust as his words are spoken, a dragon flies overhead, with a banner attached to its tail: 'THE WRONG ONE' it reads, the damning verdict struggling to be seen amidst the dark clouds and punishing Mancunian storms. 'What sorcery is this?' asks Triple Finger, pointing to the skies. Have we offended the Old God?' (He has never seen a dragon before, much less a fan-funded protest.) Triple Finger is shaking, but Moyes seems unaware of the chaos blighting his reign. 'I didn't see it,' he says, those red eyes spinning like cartwheels, 'I've been too focused on the job. Now, shall we talk summer transfers? I still quite fancy that young lad Fabregas...'

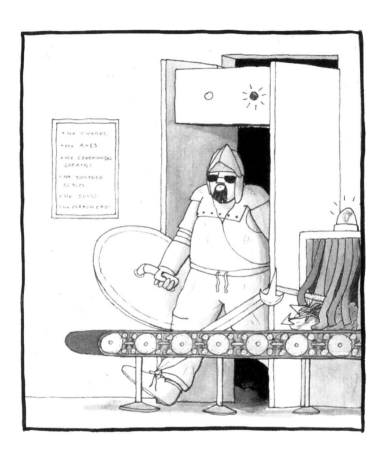

Have you got any change in your pockets, Ser?

*Chairman of the FA Disciplinary Panel hands out
a stiff penalty for misusing twitter*

44. DARK WORDS

inally Triple Finger can take no more. As the people of Mancunia batter on the doors of the castle, trying to get in and take Moyes's head for themselves, he turns over the table, all three of his heads roar with indignation, and he utters the immortal words: 'Gods help ye Davie Moyes, for now you are truly lost.' Then he straps a note to a raven which reads: 'BREAKING: House Mancunia announces that King Moyes has been banished from the Theatre of Dreams.' The raven is let fly, the peasants lay down their weapons and Moyes is dragged away by the guards. Already, it's as if he never existed.

45. THE PRINCE OF MANCUNIA

aving confessed to bringing shame on the kingdom of Mancunia, also to an unholy union with Adnan Januzaj, the once again merely Lord Moyes emerges from the torture chamber missing an arm, a leg and an ear, but wearing his usual grimace. While getting dragged away in a manure cart he reflects that, in these treacherous times, he has been lucky. Many want to see his head on a spike outside the castle gates, not least Prince Giggsy, who has been placed in temporary charge of the Knights of Mancunia, and has already started to distance himself. 'I was never Hand of the King,' he says on his first day on the Iron Throne, 'I was merely an occasional substitute. Now, loyal knights, to Norwich! Where the next battle awaits.'

46. WHAT IS DEAD MAY NEVER DIE

ut Moyes will not be silenced, not yet. Before retreating to his castle, and a massive pay-off, he pens a note to the natives of the land he so recently dared to call his own. 'People of Mancunia!' he writes. 'What is dead may never die. It only raises again, stronger. Perhaps at Crystal Palace. Or Celtic, if they give me a chance. Look at Steve McLaren! He came back to life across the narrow sea, returning with a clutch of honours from foreign lands, as well as a dodgy Dutch accent.' At Sky Sports the pundits can be heard cackling, 'You can see why they called him the mad king…'

The Dothraki Khal's refusal to cross water made travelling to European away games problematic

47. AND SPEAKING OF THE DUTCH…

hough sometimes it seems otherwise, there are many more kingdoms beyond the Twenty, on the other side of other seas. And in one such land there lives another who has also long coveted the Iron Dugout of House Mancunia. (Though for about a week he considered Spurs.) The fierce man-mountain they call Van Gaal sends gifts to King Fergie from his Orange Castle in the lowlands. Wisely, he keeps his counsel in the early days after Moyes's fall. Meanwhile, Prince Giggsy the Welsh Dragon shows promise as a future leader. Then he leads his temporary charges to a less-than-glorious defeat at the hands of the Mackem Wildlings.

48. THE PRIZE

The ultimate humiliation comes for the knights of Mancunia when Ci-teh beat Liverpudlia and House Stamford to the crown in the last days of the season, becoming Champions of the Twenty Kingdoms once again – though, as Old King Fergie can be heard cackling from his seat in the Director's Box, 'At least it wasn't the Scousers.' Perhaps, Triple Finger wonders, they have all been puppets of the Old King all along… In his cosy seat in the Director's Box, King Fergie looks suspiciously happy these days. 'Now maybe the peasants will appreciate me!' he cries out, while surveying the carnage in Mancunia, that land which has sunk so low, so quickly, in his absence.

*Daenerys Targaryen opted for her favoured attacking
30,000, 40,000, 30,000 formation*

49. THE NORTH WEST REMEMBERS

he Old God demands another cup of wine and plots his next victim, the next 'Chosen One' to whom he will gift the Throne. He picks up the phone to Holland. And so the Kingdom of Mancunia moves on to its next chapter. The Iron Throne of Games awaits a new man, Van Gaal, who names himself New King of the North and names Prince Giggsy as Hand of the King. Today Van Gaal seems invincible, but tomorrow, who knows? He too will be looked over by the stand named after the Old God. He too has Nani to rescue. Can he do it?

AFTERWARDS

ETERNAL EXILE

n these Twenty Kingdoms, men rise and men fall, and great leaders are only ever a cup upset and a couple of defeats away from being great chumps. The greatest of which, they say, is Lord Moyes, the mad half-manager now banished to the wild hills of the North West. Tonight, drunk and howling in a dingy corner of a Clitheroe tavern, Moyes think he has all eternity to imagine what might have been – but perhaps eternity awaits him sooner than he thinks. In the midst of his stupor, Moyes suddenly stands to attention, as if saluting Death himself. He calls out, 'I am the Chosen One!' Then he begins to shadow-box with the Chairman of Preston North End before falling, like a sack of horse manure, to the deck.